BEING MARRIED & LOVING IT!

A Simple Guide to *Attracting* the Relationship You *Want*
& *Wanting* the Relationship You *Have*

BENNIE CROSS

Rebirth Publications

Copyright © 2008 by Bennie Cross

ISBN: 978-09802046-0-5

All rights reserved. Printed in the United States of America.

The author freely grants permission to quote up to 300 words of this book as long as the name of the author and the source accompanies the quotation. Beyond that, no part of this publication may be produced, stored in a retrieval system or transmitted in any form or by any means, electronic, mechanical, photocopying, recording, or any manner whatsoever without the written permission of the author.

This Publication is designed to provide competent and reliable information regarding the subject matter covered. However, it sold with the understanding that the author and publisher are not engaged in rendering legal, financial or other professional advice. Laws and practices often vary from state to state and if legal or other expert assistance is required, the services of a professional should be sought. The author and publisher specifically disclaim any liability that is incurred from the use or application of the contents of this book.

If you purchased this book without a cover be aware this book may have been stolen property and reports as "unsold and destroyed" to the publisher. In such case neither author nor the publisher has received any payment for this "stripped book."

Rebirth Publications

Dedication

I give ultimate honor to my Lord and Savior Jesus Christ for which all blessings flow.

I want to thank my wife, Orletta. You are my sunshine. Your never-ending support and love is more than any man can hope to expect in a lifetime. I am so grateful.

To my baby girls Kaylin and Gabrielle – It is humbling to be the daddy chosen by God to raise such angels.

And to my heroes…people who will stand strong and fight for their beliefs – people like Gandhi, Malcolm X, Dr. Martin Luther King and Oprah Winfrey just to name a few.

My biggest hero however is alive and well. He embodies every hero into one. He lives his convictions and practices what he preaches. This book is dedicated to the man who has made me the person that I am today – my Father.

"I love you Daddy"

-Bennie III

Contents

INTRODUCTION
    Why Did I Get Married?..........................7

SECTION ONE
    Preparing for the Love of Your Life...................11

SECTION TWO
    How to Be Married & Loving It.....................33

SECTION THREE
    Crossfire – Bennie Answers Your Most Burning Relationship Questions..........................47

WHY DID I GET MARRIED?

INTRODUCTION

Having a blessed marriage is truly one of the most joyful things one can experience in life. I know that can be hard to believe in this day and age with all the failed marriages, especially in our culture. Too many of us have had marriage after marriage after marriage and still don't know what we did wrong in the first one! In saying this, I believe that there is a level of joy in life that is uniquely available only through marriage. Marriage offers the ultimate experience of companionship and commitment possible. Having someone to join with in taking care of each other can bring a joy indescribable to both of you. Marriage is having a helpmate, an encourager and support, a best friend, a trustworthy and trusted confidant. It is the experience of togetherness with someone who can you help build your career, stand with you in your challenges, create and grow up your family and affirm and pass down your family values. It is the experience of having someone tell you the difficult to hear truth about yourself with loving kindness and then stand with you in growing through change. It is having someone who accepts you naked and exposed and who doesn't take advantage of your vulnerability. In marriage there is life.

Now listen up guys…this is important…In addition to these benefits, according to research, it is very clear that marriage benefits men physically. It is a proven fact that men live longer when they are married. This is because married men generally take fewer health risks, probably due to their assuming new life roles such as father and family provider that have new, greater expectations. This implies that the influence of having someone else to whom they are responsible and accountable causes men to take better care of themselves, although *one* study found that even the life expectancy of married men who drank and smoked was longer than single men who didn't drink or smoke. Clearly, men benefit greatly by being married.

Research has further proven in general, that marriage is one of the country's most valuable resources. In support of this conclusion, one can find a wealth of evidence and information. There is a century of social science literature which reveals without fail that married men *and women* do drastically better in all measures of personal welfare then any of their unmarried counterparts. Married people live longer, they enjoy superior mental health, are physically in better health, are emotionally more fulfilled, happier, and less likely to suffer physical abuse. Studies have demonstrated that married persons are twice as likely to report being "very happy" when compared to divorced and never married. They are also 2 ½ times less likely to commit suicide than divorced and separated adults.

So, marriage has its very practical purposes.

When answering the question: why did I personally get married, I would have to say it was to garner companionship and raise a nuclear family. I'm an ole' school kind of guy with very traditional values. My wife, Orletta, and I share that belief system and make our life plans accordingly. It is my top priority to be a good husband and father. She supports those efforts and together we make it work.

Your reason for getting married or looking to get married may be different. That's fine. Whatever your goals, its most imperative to find compatibility with your mate—no one else has to agree, understand it or approve it. You and your mate are to determine your reasons and stay true to the objectives as a team, and I look forward to helping you do that!

Of course no one has the answer to all things, but I have a very successful marriage, and a good life. My lovely wife and beautiful children are happy, and none of it is by accident.

There is a systematic involvement to creating bliss inside your household. And within these pages I am going to share with you the processes that helped me achieve the marriage of my dreams. My ideas and successes are here for you as a guide. I pray that your marriage and life can be enhanced as a result of my sharing.

Preparing for the Love of Your Life

SECTION ONE

Now please hear me well. I am not a pie-in-the-sky kind of guy. I know that not all marriages have happy beginnings. Heck, they don't even have happy middles. What is not to be overlooked is that not having a happy beginning or middle does not mean you can't have a happy successful, life together. They can have happy endings. It's about the expectations and the foundation upon which the partnership is built that makes all the difference and that is something that is within the control and management of the two involved.

Clearly, everybody is not going to wake up married saying, "Oh gee, I am so happy to be married! This is the world! This is it! This is all I want in life!"

Every good, successful, happy, exemplary marriage takes time, energy and effort to develop. It involves attending to the other person to know them and learn them; who they are and what they stand for. Neither of you are going to want to do this 24/7 so expect to have struggles. Be patient with that and willing to grow in learning who your partner is. Really, you are just learning who you are also. In time, you will get to a point where you understand the other person and they understand you and the marriage will become beautiful.

According to Harville Hendrix in ***Getting the Love You Want, A Guide for Couples***, "Marriage is a psychological and spiritual journey that begins in the ecstasy of attraction, meanders through a rocky stretch of self-discovery, and culminates in the creation of an intimate, joyful, lifelong union. Whether or not you realize the full potential of this vision depends on not on you ability to attract the perfect mate, but on your willingness to acquire knowledge about hidden parts of yourself."

Okay, now I know for some of you your eyes just glazed over and you said to yourself, "Oh no. Not another pop psychology book about relationships!" Well, I'll tell you, the only thing constant in your life is you. And if there are issues in your past that have not been resolved—not just talked about, but resolved—then those are the same issues that may be keeping you from the relationship you want. It is not enough to just rehearse the issue…talk incessantly and repeatedly about what people did to you or what they said to you. You have to cut the emotional tie to the issue and enter a state of absolute forgiveness. And frankly, if you are still talking about it, it probably is not resolved. Even if you have stopped talking about it and are still not having the relationship success that you desire, there are issues to be addressed.

I know that can sound intimidating. That can sound like you'll never get to a healthy relationship. But think about it, you are the most constant thing in your life. You have been in every relationship you have ever had. And if they are not successful, maybe it is time to stop blaming everyone else for what is not working and look in the mirror. I remember a movie character called Buckaroo Bonsai (The Adventures of Buckaroo Bonsai Across the 8th Dimension-1984). One of the most memorable lines in that film was, "Remember, wherever you go, there you are." It would be a different matter if you could just set your self and all of the pain, hurt, grief, loss, disappointments, (emotional, physical, mental and spiritual) abuse, neglect, poor role models, every hurtful word, etc aside…but you can't…Wherever you go, there you are and there is all of that unresolved stuff is. And whether you like it or not, it is impacting your choice of partner and influencing who you are in your relationships. All of that is feeding your communication; what you are communicating and how. It is impacting your ability to achieve and maintain a deep level of intimacy and commitment. According to Derek Hobson and Darlene Powell Hobson in **Friends, Lovers and Soul Mates**,

"When you have developed a secure sense of your own identity, worked through some of the unresolved conflicts of childhood, feel confident and happy with yourself, and are receptive to a serious relationship, you are ready at last to make a commitment to a special person."

So, let's see, in order to have a happy marriage, one must first determine their starting point. It would be nice to say that everyone is starting at ground zero, with a blank slate, but as we have just mentioned, everyone is bringing some stuff with them from the life as it happened before the marriage relationship even begins to materialize. Please know, it is never too late to ask yourself these soul-searching kinds of questions. Just because you don't want to deal with the issues or know the answers, doesn't mean they are not still there. Sweeping stuff under the rug just makes a bump that you continue to trip over.

A good starting point is with asking yourself some challenging questions and giving some honest answers:

1. When you consider the love that you want and desire, are you really ready to receive it in your life? If not, what will it take for you to be ready? How will you know when you are ready?

2. What is your motivation for desiring a committed love relationship? What difference do you think it will make in your life?

3. How would you finish these sentences: "When I find my life partner, then I'll..." "When I find my life partner, then everything will be..." "When I find my life partner, then..."

4. What problems are you facing that you think love will solve?

5. What are you prepared to give up or take on in order to get the love you desire? What changes are you prepared to make in how you live to include your life partner? What are you not willing to change to have your partner?

6. Do you know what you want in a partner? Have you considered the characteristics you want and need in a partner? What are you willing to compromise on and what are you not willing to compromise?

7. Do you know what you should want in a partner? Are your desires based in healthy choices and desires or unhealthy ones? Are your expectations of your partner realistic?

8. *If you never found your ideal mate, would you still be able to lead a happy and fulfilled life?*

Now let's consider what makes each of these questions so important...

1. ***When you consider the love that you want and desire, are you really ready to receive it in your life? If not, what will it take for you to be ready? How will you know when you are ready?***

Often, we want what we are not ready to have and when we get it we have no idea what to do with it! It's like those people who win the lottery for a million or more dollars and in a year's time, they are more broke than they were before they spent the dollar for the ticket. They had nothing in place to manage the wealth they received. Consider that our love partner is like the million dollars and they show up in our lives only to find that we have not ended previous relationships adequately, we've not done the work we need to do to have a healthy relationship with them, or we haven't created the space in our lives for them to participate in any meaningful way. In short, we are not ready for the relationship we said we want. Get ready to receive!

So how will you know when you are ready? What does your ideal life look like with your mate? How do you spend your time? Who do you spend time with? What situations are there still to resolve in order to prevent unnecessary conflict? What relationship skills do you need to learn to be the mate your love deserves? The third step of the well-known Twelve Step program is "Make a searching and fearless moral inventory of yourselves." Be willing to see and know yourself with all the warts and blemishes you have. No one but God is perfect, so no one else should be expected to be.

2. *What is your motivation for desiring a committed love relationship? What difference do you think it will make?*

It is not healthy to expect that a love relationship will answer all of your problems. So why do you want this person in your life? Why now? What do you think you will gain by having this person? Too often we believe that our Prince or Princess Charming will save us from whatever throes of loneliness and aloneness we may find our selves in. Too often we are trying to replace a parental figure and have that person provide us with a re-parenting experience that is not their responsibility to do. Then when they fail or don't do it the way we thought they should, or, heaven forbid, have needs of their own that they want us to fulfill, we become angry and bitter. So it is important that we have a healthy motivation for wanting a committed love relationship. Otherwise, we will recreate the broken relationships of our past and continue to be unfulfilled.

3. *How would you finish these sentences: "When I find my life partner, then I'll..." "When I find my life partner, then everything will be..." "When I find my life partner, then..."*

The way you complete these sentences will indicate a great deal about your motivation. If you believe that life will be all that you want it to be... If you believe that you will not be complete until you find your ideal mate...If you are holding off really living life until you have a life partner to share it with...If you believe that your life won't have meaning until you have a committed relationship, then there is a problem. And I mean more than a little problem. Again, and I cannot stress this enough, your partner is not your salvation. They are not your completion. They are not the missing piece of your puzzle. Marriage vows say that two become one, not the half became whole. You must be a complete person in and of yourself. Then find support, encouragement, and a greater experience of yourself with and through your partner. Your partner is not your parent; they are your best friend. They are not your boss; they are your partner. They are not your housekeeper, your cook, or your provider. While each of you may occupy different roles in the relationship, each of those roles is a valuable contribution to the success and effectiveness of the relationship. Without those roles being filled efficiently, something will go lacking. The two become a greater one than they would be individually. The coming together of two is to the enhancement of both.

It is perfectly acceptable and should even be an expectation that the roles are agreed upon and not simply fallen into. Once there is agreement about the value of roles in the relationship then there can be agreement about how the relationship will function in practical terms and each partner can be valued for their contribution. Unspoken, unfulfilled expectations are fertile ground for growing a huge crop of resentment.

4. *What problems are you facing that you think love will solve?*

Sometimes the thoughts we have in our waiting time—waiting for love to come, that is—are thoughts that everything will be all right once we are married. That will be a time when finances will be great, our lifestyle will be improved, we'll know real love and have someone to share love with, we'll never argue, we'll do everything together, we'll be inseparable. Well the real deal does not look like that. The real deal is that your love partner is human with human frailties, human bodily functions, human physical needs, human emotional needs…human everything. Not to run the issue into the ground, but they are not your Savior. Unless you have hooked up with someone under extraordinary circumstances, having them in your life will not erase your debt, improve your credit, make you beautiful overnight, relieve your loneliness, clean up and organize your house, etc. etc. etc. What it will do is show you your challenges, your areas for growth, if you are willing to see them. Having your partner in your life can give you the support to make the changes and achieve the growth inwardly that you need. A healthy relationship is the arena for growth opportunities to be safely played out and experienced. Your life partner in a healthy relationship stands for your best being realized while their best is realized. They challenge you safely in ways that encourage you to take the next step upward toward your greatness. If you are not experiencing a greater sense of self, a greater expression of your authentic personhood and uniqueness, then perhaps there is some re-evaluating of your relationship that needs to take place. Please know that I am not saying here that you need to end your relationship. What I am saying is that if it is not encouraging you to be at peace, to know yourself as a worthwhile and valuable contribution, to be fully expressed as God's wonderful creation, to celebrate your strengths and be validated even inside of your weaknesses, then some new agreements need to be put in place. Nothing with God is impossible.

Your life outwardly is the reflection of your life inwardly, your thoughts and beliefs, your self esteem and your self worth. If you keep encountering the same problems with different people and different circumstances, then you have to look at what you are doing to create that situation. For instance, if you keep attracting the same abusive partner type, then there is something that you're bringing to the party that says it is okay to abuse you. Trust me, there are people in the world that never get abused and never will be because of who they are. They have it written on their foreheads, "If you think you can take advantage of me, think again and move along!" What is the message to the world that is written on your forehead?

5. What are you prepared to give up or take on in order to get the love you desire? What changes are you prepared to make in how you live to include your life partner? What are you not willing to change to have your partner?

More often than not, our partner will not just fit easily and readily into our lives. There may be some habits and ways of being that we have to adjust. When we have been living a single life for some time, we develop ways of being alone that don't work for sharing a life with someone. Then we have to be willing to let go of those ways in favor of having a different lifestyle. How willing are you to let go of what is familiar for what may be greater and not in your sight or even in your imagination with the right partner?

Be sure to notice any resentment that may come with having to change because of your partner's needs. Where have you felt that in past relationships? What relationships ended because you or your partner was not willing to change something in favor of the other person? Because of not changing, one of you felt devalued and unappreciated—which lead to conflict or the resolution of the relationship. Are you willing to let go of being right all the time? Are you willing to let go of talking more than you listen? Are you willing to allow your partner to express themselves fully, even when we don't want to hear what they have to say about how they are feeling? Are you willing not to take everything personally that your partner is disappointed about? Are you willing to change the filters through which you hear your partner and instead of hearing blame and ridicule be accountable for your part in whatever the situation is? Are you willing to let go of pride and take on humility? Often there are areas of our lives that we are blind to because they have been there for so long and were developed as the result of unresolved emotional pain. They become part of our character. They become part of who we were as we managed to navigate life through the pain all while protecting ourselves in the best way we could. Now as we seek a healthy, happy marriage, they don't serve us any longer. Are we willing to let God remove all these defects of character? What will it take for you to be ready?

6. Do you know what you want in a partner? Have you considered the characteristics you want and need in a partner? What are you willing to compromise, and what are you not willing to compromise?

Talk to most women and it seems they are looking for the ideal man…tall, dark and handsome, millionaire, muscle-bound, powerful in stature and influence, one who gets their woman-ness stirred. Most men want the ideal woman…voluptuous, beautiful, head-turner with eyes only for him, the envy of all his buddies, a wonderful homemaker, perhaps good mother material, a tiger in the bedroom (insert sound effect here—RRRRRR). Who we attract is the one who fits us. We may give good lip service about the ideal, but the one we go home to is the one who complements us. Often, if we are a "giver" by nature, we attract "takers" by nature. If we are verbally abusive, we attract someone who finds validation in being abused. If we are a substance abuser, we attract someone who is co-dependent. If we are healthy, or at least working on being healthy we attract someone who is also working on being healthy. Get the picture?

7. Do you know what you should want in a partner? Are your desires based on healthy choices and desires or unhealthy ones? Are your expectations of your partner realistic?

Do you know what a healthy relationship looks like? How will you create one? What are you doing now that is healthy and that you can continue? Where in your life do you have what you want and are you being treated the way you should be treated?

While everyone's situation is different it can still be something that offers a lesson. It can be just as helpful to know what you don't want as what you do want. You just can't stop there. Part of the reason more people don't have what they want in life is that they have never been as clear about what they want as they are about what they don't want. Approach every situation you encounter as a new opportunity to learn something about yourself and your potential marriage partner. The old saying is, "Never judge a book by its cover." Learn from it. Look and see what others are doing that is working and that is not working. There is a lot to be learned through observation, then decide what works for you and what doesn't. My father was an excellent role model. Who can you look to—if only from a far?

It can be helpful to know what a healthy relationship looks like, especially if the marriages that you have been exposed to have not been healthy.

So here are the elements of a healthy relationship vs. an abusive or harmful relationship.

Sometimes abusive relationships are easily identified. There are bruises and other obvious insults and injury; other times the abuse may be much more subtle. In general, a serious power imbalance is clear evidence of an abusive relationship, wherein the abuser controls or attempts to control their life and the life of their partner. In healthy relationships responsibility and decision-making is shared between the parties and everyone in the relationship, including children are respected. Let's start with what we don't want...an abusive relationship.

An Abusive Relationship:

Uses Intimidation as an Act of Control

- Partners make the other feel fear by using threatening looks, actions, or gestures.

- Making physical threats against one's partner or partner's family can be an element of intimidation in an abusive relationship.

- Partners may resort to a covert or overt expression of anger or rage, which may include brandishing weapons in threatening gestures.

- Partners may destroy or confiscate property and possessions.

- Pets may be abused as a threatening display of power and control.

Uses Emotional Abuse to Control Their Partner

- Unhealthy partners belittle the other and verbally put them down.

- busive, unhealthy partners disgrace and embarrass the other regularly. Nothing they do is good enough so their shortcomings and failures are exaggerated and talked about especially publicly with/to/in front of others.

- Unhealthy partners regularly and repeatedly make their partner feel bad about themselves.

- Partners harass or intimidate the other.

- Unhealthy, abusive partners call their partner names.

- Unhealthy, abusive partners play mind games making the other feel guilty for things they did or did not do. Their partner can never be or do enough to please them. And what they do is never good enough and can never be good enough.

- Abusive, unhealthy partners check up on their partner's activities or whereabouts. They want to know where they are and how each minute was spent.

- Partners humiliate the other through direct attacks or vicious, hurtful "humor" which may then be shared with others.

- Partners interrogate the other and no answer is sufficient or believed.

Uses Blame Shifting, Minimizing, and Denying

- The unhealthy partner will use jealousy to justify their actions and blame the other for making them behave the way they did. Often the comment or something similar is made, "It's your fault. I wouldn't have had to _____, if you hadn't made me! You pushed me/etc. to that level." The abusive partner rarely takes any responsibility or accountability for their actions, words or choices.

- The unhealthy, abusive partner will reduce the significance of the maltreatment to something light and meaningless, not taking their partner's feelings and concerns about it sincerely, saying the mistreatment didn't happen, or wasn't that bad.

Uses Financial Viability as a Method of Control

- The unhealthy, abusive partner keeps the other ignorant about family finances and does not allow them access to the family income.

- The unhealthy partner makes their partner ask for money, gives them an allowance and takes any money they may have.

- The unhealthy partner will prevent the other from getting or keeping a job as a means of controlling them and their activities and resources.

Uses Seclusion as a Method of Control

- The abusive partner controls what their partner does, who they see and talk to, what they are exposed to in print and the media and where they go. The unhealthy partner attempts to control every influence in the other's life as a means of controlling their life experience. This includes them limiting their partner's outside interests.

- The unhealthy partner may demand that their partner stay home. These threats are usually enforced the demand with threats.

- Along with restricting the other's outside interests and keeping them secluded and isolated, the unhealthy partner will cut their partner off from friends, family, activities, and social interaction and outlets.

Uses the Children as a Method of Control

- Partners who are abusive make their partner feel guilty about anything having to do with the children and their needs and wants, to the extent that they will even threaten to take the children away.

When the Unhealthy Partner is Male

- Some unhealthy male partners may act like they are the "king of the castle", the master of all they survey and treat their partner like a servant with servant-like expectations. Or they will make all the big decisions, claiming the woman is not smart enough to make good decisions. (Interestingly it never occurs to them that the woman chose him!)

A Healthy Relationship

A healthy relationship demonstrates and values honesty and accountability as an important part of to the relationship

- Communication between the partners is open and truthful. Past abuse is acknowledged and the partners together seek help to break abusive relationship patterns. It is important to acknowledge that abuse does not occur in a vacuum. It takes two to tango. Abuse occurs in relationship with one another and both must seek help to resolve and change the pattern.

- Each partner acknowledges use of violence and / or emotionally abusive behavior in the past and commits to changing the behavior. The result is that the behavior is released in favor of healthier relationship and communication skills.

- Each partner accepts responsibility for themselves, their decisions, their actions and their words.

- Each partner acknowledges infidelity, the trust that was broken and the effects of the infidelity on the relationship and on their partner and commits to changing the behavior. The result is that trust is re-built and the need that caused the infidelity is addressed within the relationship in a healthy manner.

- Each partner admits appropriately to being wrong. The emphasis here is on admitting appropriately to being wrong. No one is wrong all of the time and there are other issues that need to be addressed if one partner is admitting wrong doing the majority of the time.

Demonstrates Non-Threatening Behavior

- Partners talk and act in ways that cause your partner to feel safe and comfortable expressing themselves, sharing and doing what they believe and feel.

Demonstrate Respect for Each Other

- Partners listen to each other non-judgmentally.

- Partners are readily emotionally affirming and understanding of each other.

- Each partner's opinion is valued and appreciated.

Demonstrates Trust and Support of Each Other

- Each partner actively supports the other's goals in life.

- Each partner respects the other's right to his or her own feelings, friends, activities and opinions. It is acceptable for each to have activities and interests separate from the other without trust being violated.

Demonstrates Responsible, Active Parenting

- Each partner contributes to effective parenting, sharing parental responsibilities and child rearing.

- Each partner acts as a positive role model for the children. Children learn how to be men and women from their parents. Relationship patterns are taught to children and then perpetuated in the next generation. We are literally teaching the next generation how to relate to and regard each other with how we live our lives before them.

Demonstrates Shared Responsibility for a Life Together

- Distribution of work is mutually agreed upon by both partners and is fair.

- Both partners actively participate in making family decisions.

By contrast, an abusive relationship is all about controlling the other person. It generally involves an attempt to outwardly manage an internal state of chaos that can seem overwhelming by controlling all outward conditions. The typical abuser has a past experience of physical, emotional, and/or sexual abuse that is repeated in their relationships.

8. If you never found your ideal mate, would you still be able to lead a happy and fulfilled life?

The question relates to whether or not you are holding up your happiness in waiting for your Knight in Shining Armor or your Sleeping Beauty. No one is responsible for your happiness except you. If you are miserable alone, chances are you will be miserable in a relationship. Decide now that you will do what you must to attend to your own well-being and attain your own joy. You will be that much further ahead when your perfect mate arrives.

DATING

Now that we have talked about the serious stuff, I have to switch off my authoritative voice for a minute. Let's look at what you know now. You know what it takes to have a healthy relationship...you know what one looks like and what one doesn't look like. Let's talk about the process of attracting this person. Yes, I did say process. Dating with the intention to marry can be structured and result oriented. In fact, that is the best way to insure that you achieve the desired result—marriage.

It's important to go in knowing what your goals are. It is also important to make sure that you are honest about your intentions. You only want to date people who desire to get married if that is your goal. If they are in a different space in their lives—or they are looking to "have a good time"—not really settle down with anyone, etc, this person is not good match for you. The mistake that some people make going in right away is that they don't take the person's perspective at face value. Instead, they hope they can change the person's mind about getting serious and wanting to marry. This is a relationship nightmare waiting to happen! NEVER set you hopes on the expectation of changing someone.

The First Date

Okay, some people are still nervous about this. But all you have to do is be you, and be careful not to judge them. You goal this date is simply to get to know the person on a basic level. Relax and enjoy the date. You don't have to learn everything about them in one evening. You also want to show them who you really are. Being nervous may distort that image, so be the person your friends love, and you should be fine. Putting on airs will distract them from the true you, and you are not likely to get the results that you want simply because the foundation from which you started was faulty. Speaking of first dates...come see me at **www.benniecross.com**. I'll tell you all about how I met Orletta. Right now, I just want to focus on you. If I start talking about her, I will have a hard time stopping. I love that woman!!!! See...now I'm all side tracked now!!

Anyway, do what you can to spend quality time. Doing so this does not necessarily mean quality *dime*. You can get creative and recommend activities that he or she will like that does not have to be expensive. Everyone is different.

Be careful not to assume that the person wants to go to an high-priced dinner just because that is what someone did on TV or in some romance novel. Pay attention to the person's conversation. What do *they* seem to value? What sparks *them*? Are they an outdoors or indoors kind of person? Do they prefer email or telephone? What interests them—*really?* Getting a feel for these kinds of answers will give you significant insight into how to proceed. Asking questions is good. Keep communication open at all times. <u>Communication is the absolute key to successful dating, and ultimately a good life with a great love.</u>

Being honest throughout this process is important. Saying what you think someone wants to hear or simply operating in the fear of him or her not liking if they learn the truth will only postpone calamity. People who matter don't have a problem with the truth. The people who have a problem with the truth don't matter. Remember, your goal here is to be the real you. If you don't feel that the real you is good enough, you may want to engage in building self worth before trying to attract the love of your life. You will not get the quality that you deserve until you are living on the frequency to attract such quality. It's like a radio station. You have to tune the dial just right in order to connect with the clearest sound that has the strongest signal. If you are off even a little, you will not get clear music and messages. It is the same with life and drawing people into your life. You will have to raise yourself to a wave pattern of greatness in order to bring great people, situations and opportunities into your life.

Remember, while your intention is to marry—dating is still supposed to be a natural process…not a forced one. Take your time in getting to know a person. Far too often, folks are rushing into things for fear that they are running out of time. You lose so much more when you push and accelerate this process without the feelings of certainty. So pace yourself, enjoy the adventure of spending time with someone and trust the process.

Getting Engaged

When do you know when and if it is time to propose? When you feel like you will miss regret something if you spend the rest of your life without the person…When you feel your life would be better with them than without them. You may need to pop the big question. That will mean different things depending on your own person life goals and ambitions. When you come to the dating table of life with a clear sense of what makes your current life good, it is easier to determine what and who can help make that already good life even better.

How to propose is a subjective and personal event. By the time you are at this stage, you should know your mate well enough to be uniquely creative. Popping the question in a hot air balloon may be cool for photos, and a good story, but you have failed miserably if the love of your life is afraid of heights! Dropping the ring in a wine or champagne glass is not good at all if your mate is a recovering alcoholic. You get the point. So don't be so creative that you miss the real connection. What would ***your*** baby want to tell people for years to come about the day you proposed? What anyone else thinks is romantic is irrelevant. I would however, suggest that you do not make your proposal a public display.

Unless you are absolutely sure that you are going to get a "yes" you better reconsider the grand stadium announcement or the huge "down on one knee" in the middle of a crowded restaurant. You do not want to make it uncomfortable for anyone—including yourself, if the answer is not the one you had hoped for. You won't want that revealed in front of a ton of people. No matter what, if you have done your homework in getting to know this person well, whatever the answer is—it is probably the best one.

The ring is only a symbol of your love. It is not the love itself, so it's important to get what you can afford. If that is the largest jewel…so be it. But some people want the biggest ring because they equate the size of the ring with the level of love. The basis of the superficiality is not what will make a strong marital foundation. I believe that the purchaser should pick the ring. There are a couple of reasons for this.

One, when you buy the ring, you are demonstrating a very sacred act. How that act is received will be telling in and of it self. Do you really want to marry someone who would refuse you solely on the size of a ring? Secondly, if the ring is accepted and for whatever reason the wedding doesn't take place after all, the ring is hers!

Now, this is a very controversial subject. Some states require that the ring be returned or reimbursed because the contractual purpose for which the ring was given has not or will not be performed. My school of thought is that the sooner you cut loses the faster you heal and position for the right person. Giving up the symbolism of a soured engagement can be a significant gesture towards that healing. So give a ring that will not bankrupt you to walk away from. Third, marriage is a growing process. What Orletta and I decided was that our rings would grow as we do. Trade up and up. That is what works for us. Decide what will work for you and your love.

THE WEDDING

It is my best judgment that a woman should have the wedding of her dreams within the budget that you both have agreed to. If all goes as planned, this will be the one and only time she has this day, why deny her anything? Okay, the guys might be saying, but Bennie…man it's my wedding too. It is so very important to recognize that there is a societal emphasis put on the wedding day for a woman that just isn't bred into the upbringing of a man in this culture. To ignore that would be remiss. So I say that the day is more important to the woman as a general rule. Let her be queen and have her way. You will be King by default. Be there for her if she needs your help and support with planning and organizing, but for the most part let your fiancée enjoy her day…and you will undoubtedly enjoy yours. You will know you did a good job when you get to the honeymoon!

How to Be Married & Loving It

SECTION TWO

The Honeymoon

Besides the obvious honeymoon activities and purpose, now that the wedding is over, it's time to plan for your future together. I believe that in the time when you both are relaxed that you and your spouse can come together and create an outlook on how you want to live your life. Consider things like what do you want to accomplish together? In fifty years what do you want your life together to look like? What are their goals for life, what have they always wanted to do, be or have? When will you grow your family by having children? What are your long-term career plans? How long will you stay in the area of the country you currently live? Will you plan a vacation for every year and how will you finance it? How much will you place into savings each month? Cover every area of your lives together with this rudimentary plan and schedule time to revisit it every quarter or no less than once a year. It may be a great way to celebrate your anniversary each year and a great way to remember to review the plan. You can then begin your next year together by reviewing the plan and making sure you are still headed in the direction of your goals. The way to prepare for this is while the wife is preparing for the wedding, the husband can be preparing for this honeymoon conversation. First agree that this conversation will happen while you are on the honeymoon. Then write down all the areas of your life together leaving room for areas you may not have thought about. There is a sample worksheet on my website that you can use for this. Then make three copies, one for each of you to make notes on and one as a final draft. One of you must agree to complete this as a computerize, saved version when you return home (unless you've taken a laptop computer with you!). This document will be a wonderful way to start your life together with direction and purpose moving toward your goals.

Relationship skills

Every relationship, especially successful marriages, is dependent upon having great relationship skills. There are some very clear guidelines for creating and maintaining a great, happy relationship. In fact these skills are helpful even in determining that a particular relationship is not the one you want to commit to. Please know that these skills can often take time to make habit and incorporate into your given way of relating but they are well worth every minute they take to learn. Decide now that you will give them all of the energy and effort they deserve knowing that using them or not using them can make or break your relationship.

Before we actually get into the skills of relating, I think it is really important that I share a perspective with you. There is a level of relating that exists above the actual relationship. Sometimes it may be necessary to step outside of the events of relating to examine the process. Let me give you an example. Say my wife says something to me that sets me right off and I get angry. And I react out of anger. It is my responsibility to step back and look at what caused me to be so angry. Chances are my anger has nothing to do with what is happening in this moment. It may have come from something in my childhood where I didn't feel appreciated and those feelings are unresolved and showing up in this conversation with my wife. This situation for whatever reason reminds me of that on some level, probably emotional and subconscious, and I am bringing that to the present. Then, using good relationship skills, I have to go back and apologize for being angry inappropriately. Often we react to people instead of responding to them. Always the reaction come from not feeling validated, not feeling appreciated, feeling blamed and criticized, or something otherwise that needs to be healed and attended to. The extent to which we are aware of our own issues is the extent to which we can participate in a healthy relationship.

Now about those relationship skills...

These are in no discernable order. One is, no more important than the other, except communication. It is sort of the bus driver for all of the others. They're all important and the extent to which you excel at all of them is the strength you will have in the relationship. Further, the healthier both partners are inside of using these skills the stronger the marriage will be at standing the test of time.

The Skills of Relating

Avoid blaming

Part of what I said about an unhealthy relationship earlier is that it involves blaming the other person for everything that goes wrong in the relationship. It can be so easy to make your partner responsible for your disappointments and for your relationship not being what you want it to be. Great relationship skills require that each party take responsibility for their part in the relationship. If the relationship is "not working," then it is because of the union of the two. The relationship is the creation of the two and everything about it is because of how the two have come together. Avoid blaming each other for what is not working. If something isn't working it is the responsibility of both to find a solution.

Be sure that each partner feels validated in the relationship

Validation is confirmation of your partner's personhood. It is affirming them for who they are and that they are valuable simply because they exist.

A principle of validation is that each person's likes, dislikes, interests, ideas, feelings and thoughts are acknowledged by their mate.

When working on improving your relationship, an excellent place to start is for both partners to treat each other courteously and considerately. A very obvious and common form of invalidation is behaving as if the other person simply doesn't exist. I know of men who behave as if their wives aren't real. They come home and their wife is watching something on TV and just because the guy came home, they feel like they can just run things so they start changing channels. Their wives are sitting right there and the guy is changing channels like she wasn't already watching something! I think that is too inconsiderate for words! It would never even occur to me to do something like that because I love and respect Orletta.

Loving them the way they need to be loved, not the way you need to be loved or the way you need to love

Generally, when we love someone, we love them the way that we want to be loved and in the way we are accustomed to showing love. We give what we want to receive. It never occurs to us that they might not like the things we like the way we like them. The important thing is to pay enough attention to your mate and to know them so that you know what they like and don't like. That is the best and most effective way to love and the most powerful way to love. Be okay with asking the questions that will lead to a greater understanding and knowledge of your mate. Marriage is a time to learn the other person and to want to please them. You have to grow in their love language. If bringing my wife chocolate chip cookies and ice-cold milk in bed every other night says, "I love you" to her then that's what she'll get. If she likes to have her back rubbed a certain way, and that says, "I love you" to her, then that is what she'll get. We have to speak the language that speaks to our mate's heart. My wife knows that I love to have quiet time with her, just us. So because that says, "I love you" to me, she'll arrange a sitter for the kids and we'll spend an evening together, talking and connecting. It is important to remember that what we enjoy may not be what our mate enjoys. I may love to have my wife blow softly in my ear but that could be something if returned just makes her crazy with irritation! So I'm not gonna blow in her ear just because it's what I like. I'm gonna pay attention to what she likes and do that.

A suggestion to be sure that you are on the right track with making your mate feel loved is for both of you to create a list of "Things that bring me pleasure and that make me feel loved and cared about." You can start the list my completing the sentence "I feel loved when you..." Some examples may be:

I feel loved when you...
- Scratch/rub my back
- Scratch my head
- Hold me until I fall asleep
- Clean the snow from my car
- Surprise me with gifts and presents
- Wake me with kisses

- Consider me before making plans apart from me
- Give me space without feeling threatened
- Trust me
- Listen to music with me
- Sit with me on the couch while I read

Be sure to regularly include as many of the things on your list as possible in your daily lives together.

Listen with Love

In order to listen with love, you have got to let go of the filters we have in place. Those filters came from all that stuff that we experienced in life that caused us pain and hurt. It took us to a place where we expect to be hurt and then look for and prepare for being hurt. That is especially true in relationships. The intimacy of relationships can keep us on guard by exposing all of the places in us that need to be healed and that we try to protect. So when there is a conflict with our mate, we are already expecting to be hurt, blamed or criticized and we prepare to defend ourselves, even though they are not saying what we think they are. To listen with love is to listen from a place of openness without taking what your mate is saying personally. For example, your mate could be sharing with you how she doesn't feel valued and appreciated at work by her boss and how she feels taken advantage of by them. Instead of your hearing that the issue is about her boss as she has described, you go to some place in your head about how she is blaming you for not being rich enough for her be a stay-at-home mom. Listen without the filters and without the expectation, really hearing what your mate is saying and asking questions for clarification.

Communicate

Talking is easy. Communicating is a whole 'nother matter. To communicate is to exchange ideas and concepts with another in a meaningful way that assures understanding by all parties. Communicating requires greater skills than just talking does. It requires that we speak and listen with attention and skill, mindfully rather than mindlessly. Not being given over to emotions and feelings but rather being dedicated to producing an effective process of understanding together. In that process, there are certain expectations and subtleties that are important. Here are a few tips for effective communication:

- It is important that either party be free to admit that they don't have all of the answers. It is okay to say, "I don't know."

- It has to be acceptable for either party to be wrong. Pride has no place in effective communication. It contributes to a blind spot being perpetuated in the process.

- It is important for both parties to feel heard more so than to be agreed with. That understanding is communicated through paraphrasing and reiterating what the other person has shared as well as acknowledging the feelings that may have been unspoken.

- There are at least five different variations on what can possibly be communicated at any given time. That means that there are at least five different points at which communication can fail or be disrupted. They are:

1. In what the speaker actually said

2. In what the speaker meant to say

3. In what the speaker heard or thought himself to say

4. In what the listener actually heard and

5. In what the listener thought he heard

If there is a breakdown anywhere in this process, then miscommunication has occurred. At any point in this process our filters of judgments, experience, assumptions, and expectations can interfere with the communication process. Summarizing, paraphrasing and restating what you thought you heard allows the other person to correct your interpretation so that it is accurate.

For your communication to be successful, focus on common ground rather than on the apparent differences. It may also be helpful to share your intention for the communication. This gives your message a context within which the listener can achieve greater understanding easily. Remember that even though we may not be completely aware of them, we may have unspoken agendas that impact our communication. When you are doggedly defending something, ask yourself what it is that is so important that you are not willing to release even for the sake of honoring your spouses feelings?

Learn to listen well. Most people think they are good listeners when the truth of the matter is that even before the other person has finished talking, we are formulating our answer. Instead of focusing on what we are going to say next and getting our point out, we have to give all of our attention to the other person while they are speaking. Most of the arguments had in marriage are because someone didn't listen in the first place.

Celebrate your mate

I don't know anyone who doesn't enjoy being celebrated by someone they love. Take time and pay attention to your partner's likes and dislikes and plan little surprises for them. Prepare their favorite meal and place a card next to their plate or drop a love note in the pocket of their jacket or leave one in their planner telling them how much you miss them when you're apart. While they are in the shower call their cell phone and leave a message about how much you love and appreciate them. Remind them often of why you chose them and continue to choose them as your special person. Describe the character traits that you most appreciate about them and when they do something to demonstrate that trait tell them how much you love that about them.

Manage conflict before it happens

If there are behaviors or issues that you know are hot seats for your mate, determine that you will address them lovingly and compassionately. Clearly, we all still have things to heal and preferences that we want acknowledged. I would never suggest that you completely avoid difficult issues altogether, that only generates resentment and distance. However, I do suggest that with good communication skills you can join with your mate in addressing them in a healthy way together. Start with good judgment. Is the situation one that you need to be involved in at all? Before you create a situation that does not need to exist, consider your partner and their feelings and well-being. Try not be selfish. Is what you are about to do the best thing for your relationship or for just you as an individual? If there is no way around it and you now have to "come clean" with your partner, commit to being honest. Use good communication skills regarding how to share the information, where to share the information and when to share it. This is not so much an effort to manage your partner as it is to manage the situation.

Develop fair fighting skills

Fair fighting means that you stay in the moment. It is unacceptable to go back into past disagreements or disappointments and throw them back into your mate's face during an argument simply because you are angry and still angry about what happened then! No fair! Stay current and present and let the past be the past. Fair fighting means you know what the issue is and you stick to it in the conversation. Deal with each issue as it arises and resolve it, then there will be no left over stuff to go back to. That is the best way to handle every disagreement. There is the old saying that couples should never go to bed angry. While that could mean that some people would be up for days, for other couples it would be a nice reminder to waste no time addressing the issues and the feelings behind the issues. If you have not addressed the issue with your mate within the first 48 hours, be prepared to let it go. Avoid name-calling and hitting below the belt with sarcastic remarks. No teasing or hurtful humor is allowed either. Also avoid interrupting and listen openly. Avoid blaming the other and practice using "I" statements instead of "you" statements.

Fair fighting also means that you do not involve other people in the dispute. What happens at home stays at home. If you have an issue with your mate, it needs to stay between the two of you or shared only with someone who you can trust to keep it confidential and who is healthy enough to not hold the issue against your mate as fodder for future disagreements. The last thing your relationship needs is someone telling you, "See, I told you she/he was no good for you!" when you have turned to them for support.

If you are both really angry, try to hold hands and look into each other's eyes while you talk. Having such a connection can support your efforts to resolve the situation lovingly. Be willing to ask for forgiveness and willing to forgive.

Make your first desire to be at peace at all times and in right relationship with your mate. When your first desire is to be at peace, then you will be willing to do whatever you must to achieve resolution. When what is most important is that you and your mate are happy in the relationship, you have just placed your mate above anything that could come between you. That is a powerful place to start any communication from. In that space there is humility and in humility you "prefer your brother" above yourself. That means that you choose to lay your ego aside in favor of what is best for your mate and for the relationship.

Equality

While there may be different roles in marriage they are equally important for the relationship to be successful. One partner is no more important than the other. There wouldn't even be a couple without both people! How could one be less important than the other? This is a critical point in that too often in marriage women are treated as servants. Or men only contribute financially and feel anything else is woman's work. In a good marriage both men and women are considered invaluable and equal contributors to the marriage.

Partnership

This is a really important element of your marriage. The marriage should be treated like a business. I believe, like a corporation, there should be one final decision maker and that should be the husband. He is the final authority because there has to be someone with accountability for the final outcome. The decision should have been discussed and an agreement made as to what will happen, I just think it should fall ultimately on the husband to deal with any consequences of the decision. Even in a democracy, there is a president who is accountable to the people when the spit hits the fan! I think it should stay within the circle of husband, wife and children and not include outsiders. Outsiders to the marriage go home after they've caused havoc. In the end it's you and yours that are left to deal with each other.

CROSSFIRE:
BENNIE ANSWERS YOUR MOST BURNING RELATIONSHIP QUESTIONS

SECTION THREE

1. Should Children take Priority over the Marriage?

The marriage should always be the priority. It is only in having the marriage a priority that you create and maintain a healthy, happy partnership in which to raise the children. Putting your marriage first ensures that your needs as a couple are being met. Happy couples simply make better parents.

Consider this. Whenever you fly, the flight attendants routinely tell you to put your own oxygen mask on before assisting others—even children! The advice is very sound. Think about it. If you make someone else's mask a priority without securing your own, you run the risk of dying and killing him or her too! See, if while you're helping them you lose too much oxygen and die, they die also because you didn't live to finish helping them. Marriage is the same way. By keeping your marriage strong, you maintain the needed energy and stamina required for good parenting. When your marriage is healthy, you are getting what you need. When you get what you need as a person, you are then up for the job of caring for your child(ren).

2. How can I develop more intimacy with my husband? We seem to be doing alright for the most part, I just think there could be more.

Improving the intimacy starts with establishing a clear understanding of what intimacy is for the two of you. Men and women define intimacy differently. Women tend to need more tenderness, compliments, feeling heard and understood...feeling desired. Often her intimacy needs are met outside of the bedroom. She needs to know beyond a shadow of doubt that she is the only woman in your world. Some men relate intimacy with sex. As long as the sex is good they feel they are being intimate and all needs are met. But everyone needs intimacy. I want the fellas to know that intimacy is deeper than sex and goes far beyond the bedroom. The best news is that if you allow yourself to connect intimately...it definitely makes a difference in the bedroom!

Ladies, a man wants to feel that he is her knight in shining armor and that his touch is what makes his wife melt in his arms. He needs to be validated for who he is to her and how he makes her feel. He needs to know from his wife that she respects him and honors him and that he is the only one for her in her world.

The real deal is that both parties need to have their physical and emotional intimacy needs met sufficiently by their partner. There are conditions for intimacy that must be met for intimacy to be deepened between partners. They include behavior that shares their authentic self with their partner, participating in positive activities, relating positively with each other and assuring that understanding is shared and agreed upon regarding issues of the relationship. It is through the process of intimate interaction that an intimate relationship becomes distinguished from something more casual and common.

I think that deepening intimacy comes through the little gestures that we make toward each other in daily life together. These things make us feel connected to one another and help maintain the sense that we are sharing a special relationship with only our spouse. For instance, I may gently kiss my wife's forehead between commercials while we are watching TV together. Or lightly hold her face in my hands while I tell her what a phenomenal woman she is. When I know that she has had a tough time at work, I'll gently massage her shoulders and feet to soothe her. For me, I feel connected and close to Orletta when I know she is available to hear me share my dreams and thoughts with her. I enjoy knowing that while I sleep, she is close by. And it's even better for me if when I wake she is next to me just watching me sleep!

Here are some ideas about what to look for in a healthy intimate relationship:

1. In genuine love there is the freedom to share your true self with your partner and for them to share their true self with you.
2. People who love each other in a healthy, enduring way inherently acknowledge the importance of achieving individ-

ual, personal wholeness, and they know this usually comes through periods of quiet solitude and spiritual rejuvenation.

3. Being in love and having a lasting relationship involves unselfishly committing to your lover's happiness and honestly communicating your needs effectively.

4. Loving companionship requires giving trust and being trustworthy.

5. Loving companionship requires you to enjoy what your partner enjoys and willingly participate with them.

6. Successful, loving relationships involve people who share their dreams and their plans for reaching them.

7. Successful, loving, intimate relationships involve people who love each other deeply and recognize the importance of creating four spaces in their relationship – one for God, one for them as a couple, one for him, and one for her.

3. How do I stop a divorce?

When you "jumped the broom", you agreed to a lifetime of growing together. You agreed to place high regard on your life together. A marriage can only stay together as long as both partners are committed to it and willing to working on it as a natural characteristic of the relationship.

The first necessity in stopping a divorce from happening is that both people commit to seeing the marriage succeed. Although this on its own is not enough to repair a troubled marriage, it's required before anything else is possible. One partner's devotion to saving the marriage is not enough and under those circumstances, divorce is likely. Next, figure out exactly what the root cause(s) to the problems are in the marriage. In other words, discuss exactly what happened that troubled the marriage in the first place. Was a partner cheating? Were there overwhelming financial problems? Have outside influences taken their toll, like substance abuse, depression, anxiety, or problems with relatives or friends? After you know what is causing the trouble then real work begins. The problem or issue has to be addressed.

After the problem or issue has been identified resolving it and saving the marriage may require professional counseling. Be willing to do whatever you have to in order to save your marriage. Be generous with humility and large on forgiveness – only then can you say you gave your all.

Not all troubled marriages will end in divorce. On the other hand, as stats prove, not all troubled marriages will be helped either. However, by identifying the problems or issues in a marriage, and if both people are willing to work at the troubled marriage -- the vast majority or troubled marriages can be saved.

4. Can I keep my friendships of the opposite sex after marriage?

My take on this question depends on the state of the marriage and the security of the partners. If having friends of the opposite sex makes your partner uncomfortable, then cut the friend loose. Remember your goal is to keep your spouse the priority in your relationship hierarchy. Single friends of the opposite sex should ideally become friends of both you and your mate. There should be no secrets between you and your single friends. That is territory ripe for trouble and potential problems.

5. My mate and I have grown apart after a miscarriage. What can I do to bring us closer again?

Often with this level of loss it's difficult to re-group and come back together. Sometimes grief counseling is required to get past the loss of a child, even in miscarriage. What both of you have to avoid is blaming each other for losing the pregnancy. It can be really easy to fall into blaming each other or ourselves for the loss. It is a loss of expectation and hope as much as of life. Be willing to forgive yourselves and each other for whatever contribution you think was made to causing the loss. Acknowledge the feelings with each other, the grief and sorrow, the fear, anger, everything. Put it all on the table and then comfort each other and allow each other to express whatever it is that you need to in order to heal. Being available for each other this way can bring you close again. Then continue to work on developing the intimacy between you again. During this difficult time, make it a priority to count your blessings. God is good regardless.

6. I feel like I didn't choose the right mate in the beginning. Is there anything that I can do now to make this marriage work?

Begin from a place of gratitude. Without sharing yet with each other, both of you make a list of all the things you appreciated about your mate when you first got together. There were things that they did or said, or ways that they made you feel that made you fall in love with them in the first place. Now look at what you are still receiving from your mate that's on the list? Stop now and be sincerely grateful for those things. Now consider what you like to still be receiving that is on the list? What would you like to have in your relationship that isn't on the list? Are there activities that you would like to do together and ways that you can compromise to have them? Now schedule uninterrupted time – a least an hour -- to share with your mate the things that you are grateful for. Really acknowledge your spouse for how they meet those needs in your life and how grateful you are for that. Share the difference that those contributions have made to your life. Now schedule time to share the things on your list that you would like to still receive and the things that you would like to add to the list. Be willing to hear your partner and consider where you are willing to meet them in getting their needs meet and vice versa. Make an agreement that each day/week you will do something special for your mate that came from the list and show appreciation for your mate's efforts. This will revive the connection and keep the relationship fresh thereafter. Each quarter commit to coming together to check in about how each is feeling about the relationship and its progress. Be prepared to make the changes necessary for renewed and maintained intimacy.

7. I feel like my mate and I are not sexually compatible. What can we do to change that? His interests and desires are not mine.

Being certain that you know what your desires are and what his desires are then come to some compromise. Use good communication skills in reaching an agreement about what is acceptable for both of you. Listen and be heard. Be willing to come to the table with out biases. Remember, the Bible says that marriage is honorable and the bed is undefiled. (Hebrews 13:4). What you two do is your business and honored by God. Just make sure that you are honoring each other in your choices.

8. My husband works all the time and then comes home and falls asleep in front of the TV for the rest of the night. We have a great lifestyle but I'm miserable

and lonely. I don't want to look outside of the relationship to get my needs met, but I'm at my wits end and can't take too much more of this. What can I do?

It sounds to me like your spouse may be dealing with a couple of possible issues. Often men will be facing a great deal of stress in their lives and not know how to communicate that or how to deal with it effectively. The same can be true for women, especially those in high- powered executive positions. First, try to understand that your mate needs you to know what their experience is and may not be able to share it without feeling weak. Then, acknowledge your mate for their efforts in providing for the family and the lifestyle you have become accustomed to. Ask them if there is anything that you can do to make their life easier and be honestly willing to do what they say they need as long as it does not compromise your values, your safety or your self-worth/esteem. Share with them your concern for their well being without blaming them for not being available to you in the marriage. Share how much you miss spending time with them. Begin to seek compromise and set goals together for what your joined efforts will accomplish for the family. Your mate may have assumed expectations about how they have to provide that are not the same for you. You may be placing a higher priority on their mental, emotional and physical health than you are on having a mansion and wearing designer clothes. Agree on where you are headed as a family, as a couple financially, emotionally, intimately, and in every other aspect of your lives then put some timelines in place. Revisit the deadlines along the way to assure that they are still active. You can agree that if the goal is not achieved by the deadline, then you will create a new goal based on the family values, one that keeps your family healthy and happy and gets everyone's needs met.

9. Is it ever okay to make work a priority, even for a while, if we have a goal in mind and are working together toward that goal? My concern is that once we have reached the goal we will have grown so far apart that the marriage suffers.

It is okay to make work a priority as long as there is a definite end in mind. It is not acceptable to make work a long-term priority in place of dealing with issues you want to avoid at home. As long as there is an agreed upon goal with a deadline/timeline and plan for goal achievement make the sacrifice. In the meantime, continue to plan and share intimate time together however brief to maintain the connection and commitment to the goal. Plan ways to celebrate the achievement of the goal and look forward to celebrating together that accomplishment.

10. My husband says that I spend too much time with my girlfriends and other activities away from home. I enjoy those activities and don't want to give them up. I don't want him to feel ignored, but I don't want to give up what I'm doing. How can we find compromise?

It's not necessary for you to completely give up your friends and the time you spend with them. It is healthy for couples to have outside relationships/friendships. It's absolutely healthy to want time away from your mate. It assures that each partner can maintain a healthy sense of self and independent interests. No one should be all things to all people and with your partner as your primary relationship there needs to be room for each spouse's needs are met appropriately through friends, other family members, and other activities. Encourage your mate to have friends and activities apart from you as well. It can help each of you be a happier, more rounded and interesting companion. You will have to find ways to make your mate feel important and chosen by you. Be willing to schedule time with your mate just like you schedule time with your friends. Plan dates like you did before you married. Be willing to reduce the amount of time you spend with them in favor of renewing your friendship with your mate. Nothing should be more important than your connection with spouse.

11. *When I try to share my feelings with my mate, s/he turns a deaf ear and tells me it's all in my head and that I shouldn't feel the way I do. How can I get through to him/her that I'm hurting and I can't go on with this too much longer?*

To start with, be sure that you are clearly communicating your pain. Have you point blank said to your partner, "I'm hurting and I need to talk to you about why I'm hurting?" Then calmly and without blaming him/her for your pain, explain the situation and circumstances that brought you to this point without babbling and running on unnecessarily. Say clearly what the issue is and use good communication skills to share it. Practice before you actually talk to your husband so that it sounds clear. Then invite him in with his opinion on a solution to the problem. Nine times out of ten women talk and talk and talk which begins to sound like the adults in the Peanuts cartoons to men, "whaa, whaa, whaa, whaa." It becomes noise that men just want to avoid so they turn a deaf ear. Also avoid blaming him for the problem. It took both of you to create the situation and it will take both of you being committed to finding a solution together. Schedule uninterrupted time to talk. Your marriage is important to both of you and deserves specific time set aside to address the issues. Also know that your spouse may feel ill equipped and challenged to deal effectively with what is bothering you. Be willing in the process to get some help together and to reassure him/her that you believe the issues can be resolved together. Remember s/he needs to know that s/he is still your number one choice.

12. My mate refuses to spend time with the children and me. Even when we do things that I know he enjoys he will not join us. How can I get him to want to be involved with us?

Ask him what he would enjoy doing with you as a family and then schedule that event according to his availability. Be willing to do things that he wants to even if you don't enjoy the activity as much as he does. Make sure he knows how much you and the children value and enjoy his company and companionship.

13. My wife is wonderful but I'm not very creative. I would really like some suggestions on what I can do to show her how much I love her beyond just giving her cards and flowers.

Find out some of the things that she enjoys and values. Listen to her conversation. Chances are she is telling you what she would like. Both of you can create a list of things that you would like to receive from your mate and exchange lists. Use that information to surprise each other with exactly the things already identified on the list. That way you can't go wrong in knowing what pleases your mate. Leave room for new things to be added. Learn to simply pay attention to your mate and hear what they are passionate about. Actually take time to talk with each other sharing what activities you enjoy.

14. I have an extraordinary husband. He is the man of my dreams. The only issue is that he spends more time obsessed with sports -- playing and watching

-- it seems to have taken a priority over being with me. I've tried spending time with him doing what he loves to do but that is getting old, especially since the effort does not seem to be appreciated and returned. What can I do to get his attention back?

Just a suggestion, if he is home watching the game alone, purchase a jersey from his favorite sports team and wear it during one of the games. Add some stiletto heels, sexy lingerie, and perfume. During the commercial breaks, bring him snacks and other "refreshments." You then become part of the festivities at half time. Eventually, your husband may choose to miss a game in favor of engaging in "other activities," if you get my drift. Have you shared with your husband that you want his company in some of your interests? Too often we assume that we have shared our desires only to find out that when we speak directly, our spouse had no idea what we had been trying to say all along.

15. I keep choosing the same guy over and over again and getting my feelings hurt. It always ends up with me ending the relationship and being alone again. I'm just about to swear off of dating ever again. Is there hope for me ever meeting the right one?

In order for you to attract the mate of your desire, you must become the mate you desire. You need to work on yourself to become the best you that you can be. As you work on your self-improvement, you will then attract a different level of companionship. You need to be the "good thing" and he'll find you. (Proverbs 18:22) Were I single, I would consider using a dating service as a way to meet new people. Visit **www.benniecross.com** for more dating service information.

16. How can I keep my in-laws out of our marriage? It's ruining us. My husband/wife asks them for their opinion about every decision we make, even after we have agreed about what we will do.

Therefore shall a man leave his father and his mother, and shall cleave unto his wife: and they shall be one flesh." Gen 2: 24. There should be no outsiders making decisions in your marriage. You have to have a conversation with your spouse about what his/her actions are doing to the marriage and how they are affecting your relationship with your in-laws. This requires your honest sharing of your feelings and concerns with your mate. S/He may not be aware that the situation is affecting you. You are responsible for sharing what you feel rather than expecting your mate to read your mind. If you find yourselves in heated discussions or arguments, then be sure to use the rules for fair fighting. This is not necessarily an impossible situation -- though depending on your spouse's attachment to his/her family, which sounds pretty tight, s/he could feel threatened and at a loss when you indicate your need to keep your decisions between you. Be sure not to blame your mate for involving his/her family. S/He may be insecure in making decisions and thinking s/he's doing what is best for the family. Try to hear your mate out and understand the motivation for involving the in-laws.

17. I love my wife, but she puts me down all the time. I can never get anything right no matter what I do or how hard I try. How do I gain back my dignity and her respect?

First know that people who are emotionally hurt -- hurt other people. Generally when this kind of thing is the case, somewhere down the line, your mate was hurt by something you did or said and she never got over it because it was never fixed. Perhaps she never communicated to you that something was wrong or maybe she did and you didn't hear it. You must find out what caused her to lose respect for you and be willing to hear the truth. You must put your biases to the side, and hear her pain. After she has emptied herself out to you, you have to take reasonability for the part you've played in helping her to feel the way she is feeling. You must be willing to reach the depths of her pain with a heart-felt apology. That will gain her respect and you'll get your dignity back. The worse thing you can do is defend your position and blame her for the break-down. This will only make matters worse. She will feel hurt all over again as though the situation took place an hour ago. Effective communication is the key to any successful relationship. You must also be willing to do whatever it takes to get back into right relationship with her. Start with humility and a willingness to meet her in her pain. If you are not willing to do this you may be positioning your relationship to grow further and further apart.

18. I am thinking about having an affair. I don't want to ruin my marriage, but I am desiring someone who is desiring me – unfortunately it's not my spouse. What do I do?

In this situation it is critical that you share your feelings with your spouse. Discuss the needs that you have which are not being fulfilled in the marriage. These unfulfilled needs are moving you to want to have the affair. Honest, open and sincere communication is necessary. Share with your spouse what you need to feel whole. Create a safe place in which you can both feel comfortable and protected enough to share your true feelings. Avoid blaming, judging and criticizing, rather share the responsibility with your spouse for having created this situation together. It will take both of you to resolve it. Be willing to be wrong and compromise. Whatever you do. Don't have an affair. Resolve your issues with your mate or let them go altogether, but there is never a good reason to betray your vow...ever!

19. My wife earns more money than I do. She is not hounding or using it against me. I know that I shouldn't be bothered by it, but I am. How can stop feeling threatened?

Decide to change your perspective. It sounds like your wife is working with you as a team though you are experiencing her as being the competition. Remember that once you came together in marriage, you became one. What is hers is yours and what is yours is hers. Develop gratitude for the resources she is bringing to the marriage and that she is not throwing it in your face as other wives have done to their husbands. Share your feelings with your wife and elicit her support for your being secure about finances in the marriage.

20. I have developed a very comfortable single lifestyle, and I don't know if I have emotional or even physical space for anyone else at this point? How do I scoot over and make room in my life for someone else?

First you have to be clear as to whether or not you want someone else in your life or are you being influenced by society to want someone. If it is sincerely your desire and not someone else's for you, then begin to look for ways that you would include someone else. It can be as simple and profound as sleeping on one side of the bed rather than in the middle. This begins to open room for your mate to "show up" and fill that space. Do things that you may be avoiding because you don't want to do them alone, like going to the movies or dinner. If it is something that you might do with a partner, begin to add those activities to your lifestyle. You would be amazed at what a difference these simple things can do. You are essentially beginning to act as if you already have a mate. You must shift your thinking to reflect having a mate. Catch your thoughts. When you consider having a mate in your life, be grateful for them rather than wishing for them. Gratitude implies that you already have what you want. Wishing implies that you still don't have it.

21. My man has major baggage – baby mama drama, misbehaved children... just baggage. I love him, but I hate that his past spills into our future together. What can I do now?

Remember, when you signed up for the relationship, you knew that he had baggage. Don't act brand new now. You have to get back to the patience and understanding that you had when the relationship was new. Be willing to communicate your concerns about the drama to him, not blaming or making him feel bad about past decisions. State your concerns lovingly and with a willingness to find a resolution. Develop a plan together that works for both of you. Be willing to allow him to have a relationship with his children and their mother(s) regarding the best interests of the children. You can support him without supporting the drama. Be able to separate the "baby-mama-drama" from your husband's intentions. Together you can create healthy boundaries that work for everyone.

22. Every time my wife and I have an argument, she gets her mother involved. She complains to her about me. When I am around her mother I then get the cold shoulder even after my wife and I have made up. How can I get my wife to stop talking about us to outsiders?

Don't wait to tell your wife how much you don't appreciate her involving her mother when you're angry at each other. Sit down and have a discussion on how both of you together can come up with a healthy way to resolve your issues without outside influence. Tell your wife how you feel when she talks about you to her mother and how it affects your relationship with her mother. Avoid blaming her for wanting her mother's support. If she has a positive relationship with her mother, she is used to getting support from her. Keeping your issues between you will be new and maybe difficult for her to do initially. Somewhere along the way in the your relationship together, you developed a communication style that made it okay to include others in your relationship, or there was no place created safe enough to share your feelings without outside validation. If the relationship is important to your wife, help her see how hurt you are by her involving her mother and validate her need for support. Together you can establish new ground rules for communication and new levels of intimacy that validate both of you.

23. My mate had an affair and now there is a child. I don't want to end this marriage, but this has got to be one of the hardest things I've ever had to deal with. How do I accept this and move on?

If you truly are committed to maintaining the marriage, then you have to reach an authentic place of forgiveness and be willing to let the infidelity and hurt go. Stop seeing the child as a representation of betrayal and decide to see the child as representative of something that was missing in your relationship. You have the power to make the relationship better and address the issues that led to the infidelity in the first place. Remember that the infidelity was not about you. Somewhere, somehow the person who was not faithful felt inadequate, unappreciated and not valued. They then took those feelings and made a bad decision to get those needs met outside of the marriage. This may require professional counseling to resolve; so be willing to do whatever is necessary if you want to save the marriage.

24. I bought this book because I feel pressured to get married even though I really do love my life as a single woman. Everyone tells me that I am going to regret not getting married. I really don't feel I will regret anything. How do I get folks off of me?

I respect a person who has created such a great life that s/he is whole and complete in and of himself. Remember, you are leading a full life because you developed the confidence to do so. It will take that same strength and confidence to stand tall for the life you built when others come against it. You don't have to explain, apologize or defend your happiness as a single person. You don't need approval to be content with yourself and your singleness. People who are happy in their marriages don't generally feel a need to recruit others. It is my experience that the folks who are lonely and incomplete in their own choices seek comfort in enlisting other people. Don't be swayed. Be happy. If you choose to stay single, do so on your own terms. If you choose to marry do so on your own terms. Whatever you do make sure it's for you.

25. How do I know if my mate is on the "down low"?

One thing to look for is for is extreme homophobic behavior. If your mate grows emphatically outraged when confronted by anything related to homosexuality it might indicate that your spouse is gay or bisexual. This won't make sense at first glance, but deeper research will explain why. If you suspect it, do some additional homework.

If your husband or wife continually "bashes" or takes digs at gay related issues and lifestyles or if s/he is furious at anything concerning homosexuals or homosexual behavior, let that be a warning. Of course, s/he may just be very much opposed to the gay lifestyle, but being obsessive about it can be a sign. Being excessively repulsed is unnecessary when you are a sexually secure heterosexual person.

Your mate may also be receiving an inordinate amount of phone calls from one person in particular. If it is a person you do not know or a man that your husband does not willingly bring to your attention (such as an old friend from high school who happened to get in touch with him), be concerned.

Men folk typically hang out in a group. Too much alone time with one man in particular is a sign that perhaps your husband is on the "down low". At the very least, you can suspect that he is involved in a level of intimacy that could be shared with you. Trust your instincts in this situation. If you really feel as though something strange is going on, there is probably a legitimate reason.

Another sign that may suggest you have a down low husband is if your mate loses interest in you sexually all of a sudden. These are not the same tendencies of women. Women spend alone time with other women and lose interest in sex with their husbands for various reasons that may not suggest they are homosexual. If your husband is difficult to arouse or seems to be on another planet mentally during intimate moments, look into it.

Also, uncontrollable womanizing may not be what it seems. While it may look like your husband can't get enough of women, it may just be that he is trying to avoid, or stamp out a subconscious desire for a man. This is not necessarily the case for all men who have extra-marital skirt chasing issues, but again it's worth checking out if you already have suspensions.

26. My mate is obsessed with her weight. I love her the way she is, but she isn't happy with herself. How do I convince her that I love her, and still find her attractive?

The answer to this has to come from your mate. You can tell her all day long how beautiful she is to you and if she doesn't believe you it won't change a thing. She has to do the work to improve her self-esteem and with your continued support she can. Have you heard the saying, "A mind convinced against its will is of the same opinion still?" She has to change her mind about her self-worth and beauty. A suggestion for you both is to engage in a self-esteem building activities. Listen to self esteem tapes and CDs. She has to change her body image to a more positive one. Support her if she wants to make improvements. Work out with her, change your eating habits together. I would also mention here that it is common for women in our society to believe that unless they reflect what the media and common culture says is beautiful they are not. Black women in particular have struggled with this until recent years. Also, be certain that your wife is not suffering from a potentially serious mental health concern regarding her body image. Anorexia Nervosa and Obesity are serious health issues in our society and should not be taken lightly. Get your wife professional help if it seems to progress beyond what is reasonable and healthy.

27. My mate has let himself go. I don't find him attractive at all. I know that I should love him the way he is, but I just don't. What now?

You have to be honest with him about how you feel. It sounds like the way he looks now is not where you started out together. Barring any serious health challenge that contributed to his condition, there can be emotional needs that he is trying to meet with food. State your concerns lovingly and ask him how you can support him. Chances are he's not happy with the changes that have occurred either and may feel powerless to do anything about them. There are many programs that support diet and exercise, etc. Join one with him and together make the changes in lifestyle that he needs to get healthy again. If the problem is hygiene oriented, there are programs that can address the emotional issues that caused these problems in the first place. Be gentle with your husband as he begins to deal with these potentially difficult self-esteem and self-worth issues.

28. My wife earns more money than I do. She uses it as a weapon when we argue. It makes me feel less than a man. What can I do besides earning more money?

The issue isn't really about money at all. Evidently in the argument your wife feels powerless on some level and feels like she has to hit below the belt to gain ground. This means that when you are not arguing you need to develop a different style of communicating and when you do have a disagreement, you need to follow the rules of fair fighting. Work on communicating with respect and honesty as a natural part of your relationship. Agree that when you disagree, you will consciously follow the rules for fair fighting which includes not hitting below the belt, not blaming, criticizing, name-calling, bringing up the past, using or one's weaknesses or challenges against them. Agree to stick to the subject and commit to resolution together.

29. My wife lives at church. I don't particularly care for her pastor. I think that she is spending too much time away from home. I don't think you have to go to church 24-hours a day to please the Lord. How do I say this without looking like I don't want her to serve God?

Since you don't particularly care for her pastor, maybe you need to suggest praying together about finding another church that both of you can attend together. Be able to lead her in prayer. This may take some preparation and growth on your part if you do not feel equipped to do this. You may have to visit other churches on your own, find one that provides services that speak to your spirit and invite her to attend. Make sure the church is one that supports and encourages family togetherness away from the church. Too often men just want their wives to give up church without providing any alternatives. Share with your wife ideas for what you would like to do together. Also consider that the issue may not be about the church she is attending as much as it may be about your feeling neglected. Be someone she wants to spend time with and she may make the choice to be with you more often. To do this you will have to do the intimacy work that deepens the connection between you and improves communication.

30. My husband promised to stop cheating, but he keeps doing it. I love him,

and I still want to make this marriage work. How do I help him keep his stuff in his pants!

This takes a strong commitment to your marriage on both parts. You need to be clear whether or not your husband is as committed to making the marriage work as you are. If he isn't, then you are spinning your wheels. If he is willing to save it, then my suggestion is that you seek counseling. There are issues going on that you need support addressing since he cannot seem to stop the behavior on his own. There may actually be an addiction to sex in the works here.

31. Help Bennie! *My mate spends like we are rich. I love nice things too, but we are in over our heads in debt. How do we get a grip on our money?*

I recommend that you put some new agreements in place concerning your finances. You can set an allowance aside for each of you to use monthly making sure that your household commitments are being met. Then look at reasons behind the spending. Is she trying to get emotional needs met through spending? Is he substituting the attention he needs from his wife by spending? There could be many reasons that the spending is taking place and those issues need to be addressed as a couple.

Got more questions?
Need more answers?
Stop by and ask me at **www.benniecross.com**

Remember, if you are with someone everyday, you are bound to have an argument about something over time. Please know that arguments can be a good thing on some level. Try to think of arguments as cleaning pipes that flush systems to their point of clarity. With all things out in the open, you clearly have a fresh start to recover and reconcile.

I believe that being happy 99% of the time is possible and an art form. It is something that you and your spouse can work towards and grow to. I don't believe that it is possible to achieve however without growth, communication and commitment. Once you learn yourself and your partner, you know what to expect. Embrace your commonalities and your differences. Keep the channels of communication open with honesty as the chief principle to the fabric of your relationship. Above all, have faith and maintain a strong foundation in Jesus Christ. Be blessed in wedded bliss. My family prays every good thing for your family, and I look forward to hearing about your happiness. Until next time...live well.

Become a Bennie Cross VIP Club Member!

Receive my FREE *Empowered Family*™

e-zine tips

These golden strategies will provide practical insight

For achieving your relationship goals!

Sign up now at:

www.benniecross.com